Weave A Poem

... wife who joyfully
..... my occasional isolation and marriage to
my computer but with even greater enjoyment
appreciates the results and gives encouragement.

CONTENTS

MY WIFE

I'm lucky I have the most wonderful wife,
She's my friend, and my lover, she's the whole of
    my life,
She's so gentle and kind with no faults I can find,
And our grandchildren just love her to pieces.

She's a real super Mum to our daughters and son,
As companion she's certainly second to none,
She loves rabbits and dogs, ducks, swans and
    black mogs,
Beavers, otters and little white meeces.

She's an outstanding cook, and enjoys a good
    book,
She loves sewing and plants that she's growing,
She loves mountains and trees, sand dunes and
    the seas,
But the best thing of all – SHE LOVES ME.

I'm proud of my wife, she's the whole of my life,
And at some time, if we're parted for ever,
I will just pine away, from the very first day,
Till the day that we're both back together.

AGE ADVANTAGE

Getting older may worry, so set an example,
The following 'Pluses', are just a small sample;
Developing warts and brown spots which aren't
    cute,
Won't worry you too much, you can't see the
    brutes.
You wait for replacement of hip, heart and knee,
And National Health glasses are needed to see,
'When I was your age' is in regular use,
To the young who are now hooked on hard drug
    abuse.
The cost of good face creams to clear up your
    spots,
No longer concerns you, although you've got lots.
A fear of the dentist's a thing of the past.
In the evening, you put your two sets into glass.
Hairstyles may change from the short to the long,
You've no need to worry 'cos yours has long gone.
You'll cause consternation at the songs of today,
As you locate Bing Crosby's old records to play.
You have to wear bands round your wrists and
    your knees,
And exercise daily or your old joints will seize.
Your Zimmer frame's slow, so it's now motorised,
As you flash past the shoppers, they all look
    surprised.
Your toupee needs tinting, what's left is now
    white.
Always take Brufin and Zantac each night,
Keep taking your tablets; you're addicted to none,

But can't do without them, at least not for long.
When your children are married and have children too
You can pass on your knowledge if they've not a clue.
You welcome your grandchildren into your home,
Then pack them off quickly if they start to moan,
Some say that the angels have harps and two wings,
But best to keep living, have fun and some flings.

FORTY YEARS

It was only around 1950, that I started to note my
    surrounds,
Recording events as they happened, in my diary,
    which is leather bound,

The year 1950, I'm sure, was when Sainsbury's
    did build London's store.
'51 and meat rations were poor, just four ounces
    you got and no more.
'52: and no clatters or clangs, as London said bye
    bye to its trams.
T.V. Commercials in '53, were not as professional
    as those we now see
In year '54 we saw 'Flashers' galore, on cars, bus
    and trucks. It was law.
Now 'H' bombs we made in year '55, just to
    'ensure that we all survive'.
The year '56, Makarios with tricks, was deported
    because of his lies.
'57 to Heaven Jodrell Bank's largest scope gave
    stars a really good poke.
'58 wasn't great, parking tickets if late and
    motorists got into a state.
'59 was O.K. as the first motorway, opened round
    Preston they say.
In '60 it's clear, National Service still here, will
    cease by the end of the year.
Contraceptive by mouth, in year '61, and
    unwanted births will be gone.
Pandas were crossing in year '62. No need to

worry, they're only for you.

'63 with its millions, from Royal Mail, no one is caught or put into jail.

Death penalties quashed, in year '64, creating more problems, in future I'm sure.

'65 saw the motorists feeling quite sore as maxi speed 70, was the new law.

'66 and we saw, North Sea gas come ashore and now they're searching for more.

'67 we did see 'News at Ten' on T.V. and colours of which there are three.

September of 1968, approved two tier stamps for your postal rate.

1969 was great as Great Britain's Concord was 'Bang' on that date

1970 was a very good year as Pan Am's first Jumbos are landed here.

'71 was quite good for the 'Bear', as decimal coinage filled the air.

'72, is known as 'Coal Ration Year' as the striking Miners' claims become clear.

A General Strike in year '73, nearly brought Great Britain down onto its knees.

'74 and we saw Industrial peace, with Miners' wages a one third increase.

The House of Commons in '75, is broadcast to our Nation and it's live.

And then in 1976, Traffic Law stated seat belts must clunk click.

Laker's new Jumbos took off in this year, so '77 flights were not quite so dear.

In '78, Cambridge challenges late, it sank just one

mile to the finishing gate.

In '79 we appear 'Hell Bent' as we suffer a 'Winter of Discontent'.

1980 did prove that the SAS 'can', they got out those held by the men from Iran.

At fourteen hundred and ten metres long, the Humber bridge opens in year '81.

No one in Britain believed it was true but our Falklands war was in year '82.

'83 Maggie Thatcher takes over control, inherits 3 million now on the Dole.

Comedy's set back in year '84 as Eric of Morecambe will amuse us no more.

'85 is the year for Sir Clive's 'mean machine' or is it C5 electric machine?

'86 and the Chunnel gets its 'Go Ahead'. 200 years of arguments dead.

October of 1987, Stock Exchange collapses as we all pray to heaven.

Lockerbie tragedy, in '88. The world demands justice for which we must wait.

It's the turn of the Commons for T.V. this time, with televised actions in '89.

1990 the Government's not pleased, they have to admit our cows are B.S.eed.

Each year I could mention a whole list of things, but why don't we wait and see what they bring?

THE ALTERNATIVE LIFE

I'm old and grey and a proud 'Wrink – a – lee',
I've got arthritic joints in my elbow and knee,
If a tap were to drip, or there's some water surge,
Then I hope there's a loo to relieve my dire urge.

My brain is still active, I play whist, bridge and
  chess,
It's the rest of my body that seems such a mess,
I have to wear 'specs' to locate reading glasses,
My memory's failing, but returns in short flashes.

The cost of our heating, house rates and the lights,
Means we go without food to get out of our
  plights,
When putting my pants on there's plenty to spare,
But it no longer matters as there's no one to care.

My arthritic knee needs elastic support,
And the tip of my nose sports a silly great wart,
My teeth are ill fitting and they click like maracas,
But the wife says at my age new teeth would be
  crackers.

The weight of the candles on our birthday cake
Sets the fire alarm ringing and the table legs break.
We've a wonderful daughter who does all she can
To keep our place tidy, and all, spick and span.

Our medical chest in the bathroom's too small,
Our numerous prescriptions won't fit in at all.
We'll forget all our worries, the woes and the
strife,
We don't really fancy 'THE ALTERNATIVE
LIFE'.

CARAVANNING

This year, we hired for holidays, a caravan we'd
    never used,
There was me, my wife, my Mum and Dad and
    Grandma, who's confused,
On site, the car bogged down three times which
    caused old Gran to moan,
We'd only been on site an hour and I wish that
    we'd stayed home.

The girls had not used calor gas, so our dinner
    was overcooked,
And the frig they said was solid ice, a thing we'd
    overlooked.
My Dad and I got the awning out, we didn't have
    a clue,
With all those tubes we got confused so packed
    that job in too.

The frig had split the eggs apart and the butter
    wouldn't spread,
'Oh heck,' I thought, 'This is a mess, we're
    reduced to jam on bread.'
As darkness fell on the Caravan Park, we switched
    on the ceiling light,
But as we had no mains supply, we all got an early
    night.

As we all lay there in the dark, suddenly Grandma
    spoke,
'A glass of water for my teeth, or surely I will
    choke.'

9

'Oh give them here,' my Dad did sneer, 'I'll put
  them into water,
But why on earth, it should be me, I wish we
  hadn't brought her.'

With tap turned on, no water came, the battery
  we'd left at home,
Dad went outside, we heard a thud and then a
  horrid moan.
Dad dropped Gran's teeth in oozing mud, six
  inches deep all round,
Whilst Mum in van, wondered how her man
  produced a squelching sound.

So there we were at twelve o'clock scrambling
  round like water hogs,
To find Gran's top and bottom set buried
  somewhere in the bogs,
Without a light we felt around, up to our necks in
  mire,
Gran struck a match, there was a flash and the
  caravan caught fire.

Then Granny said, 'Forget my teeth, because
  we've got no food,
And by the way you look so daft stood there
  completely nude.'
The caravanners rallied round, they brought
  chicken and sausage too,
We thought they'd come to help us out, but they'd
  come for a Bar-B-Q.

The van burnt well, the food was good,
Burnt sausages with a hint of wood,
I'll tell you now, when we get home, caravanning
    we'll reassess,
I'm going to take up tiddlywinks after witnessing
    this mess.

IT'S A DOG'S LIFE

When I was a puppy and very young,
I'd tear round the house and have great fun,
I'd widdle up the sides of chairs
And do my doodies everywheres.

When morning mail came through the door,
I never let it touch the floor,
I'd rip them open in a flash,
Converting letters into trash.

But the greatest fun throughout the day,
Were evening papers that came my way,
For some strange reason it's not found funny,
Dad went ballistic and so did Mummy.

As I grew older and learnt House Rules,
I no longer pooped and made large pools,
I'd take my Dad out on his lead,
Around the park to fulfil my need.

I'd attach his lead to my collar loop,
He always brings my pooper scoop.
I'd take him walkies when he's ready,
Or perhaps a jog that's nice and steady.

If he was good I'd release his lead,
The gents' loos near, which he's sure to need,
The local pub is quite near here,
I'd wait outside while he slurped a beer.

Then once back home in my easy chair,
You know, the one I let HIM share.
I'd ask him nicely for my meal,
Then lick his face with considerable zeal.

You've got to give my Dad his due,
He often tells me 'I love you'.
I never mention the Rose and Crown
To Mum, who'd think he'd let me down.

Every day that Mum grooms me,
She shares her biccies afternoons with tea,
And when she goes off into town,
I select my chair and snuggle down.

Human beings have the strangest features,
It's hard to train such stubborn creatures,
You'll never be at a serious loss,
Once THEY understand that YOU'RE THE
    BOSS.

EL NINÔ

You all must have heard of El Ninô's effect,
It's depositing oceans on land,
The tornadoes that follow are quite scary too,
As your home turns to rubble and sand.

If El Ninô should flood us in Britain today,
Would the 'Right type of water' appear?
Would Insurance decide that their policy's void
As such floods don't appear every year?

When forced from your home, could you all keep
afloat?
Survival would be your concern,
Where do you think that you would find a boat?
Or could you just wait for 'Your Turn'?

Yellow Pages could help to find boats 'Off the
shelf',
At a D.I.Y. shop or main store,
With their brochure, a tape and a plan of their
boat,
Could you really ask them for much more?

So off you would go to the D.I.Y. store,
Once you knew that they'd got boats galore,
When you get to the store, there'd be arrows I'm
sure,
To guide you to boats on the floor.

You should go on a Wednesday to get ten per cent,

There's no point in wasting your money,
If you check the whole kit you'll find parts that
   don't fit,
And the Taiwan instructions look funny.

You would leave the whole lot when you see what
   they've got
With instructions in Taiwan and Jap,
You would wade homeward bound in a
   disgruntled mood,
And watch tele or go for a nap.

If El Ninô should flood us in Britain today,
And your D.I.Y. store had 'those boats',
Just sharpen your pencil and draw up your plan,
Make your own boat and hope that it floats.

*Where you see D.I.Y. this is NOT to be read as Do
it Yourself.*

EDUCASHUN

No won wud beleev it, but wonce I cudn't spel,

The meening of long wurds, to mee, was a
misteree as wel.

To understand the noospapers or buks was very
hard,

I tride to teech miself at home from all those
pikchure cards.

A naybore hoos a teecher, sed that shee wud soon
teech mee,

Reesults of her good teechings is wot yoo will
now see.

My bruther got sum Hard Red wud, that's cawled
MANOGAMEE,

Hees made a luvly CRIPT, he says, for sisters new
babee.

My sister in ETERNITY, got a shoker, in her ward,

The little won was stil atached to her
DIABOLICAL cord.

My Muthers hiley qwalifide, shee's a BANISTER
of lore,

Its nown that shees solicited for twenty yeers or
more.

Shee says the best DETERGENT is to lok up gilty
wons,

Then thro away the kee, shee sez, just like in old
daze gons.

Shee sufers from SUPRESHUN and SKEPTIC
ulcers too,

A DISCRIPSHUN from her docter, was 'Antacids

that yoo choo'.

My farthers bruther's got a car, hee kept the thing outside,

Hee got a SEXUAL garage, in too witch his car cud hide.

My farther has got ASTEROIDS, or so the docter says,

Hees also INCONSISTENT, in his toyletaryways.

Hees problems with his PROSTRATE, or so my muther sed,

Hee wont get up til lunsh time, hee just lies there in his bed.

He has to use DEPOSITREES, at leest three times a day,

ABOMINABAL panes, hee says, then qwickly fade away.

Hees always waching futball, with keen interest in the scaw,

Last week his teem from Fife scord five and Forfar only for.

So now that I can reed and rite and yoos big wurds aswel,

I'm going to rite a bloc buster, I'm shure that it wud sel.

So wish mee luk.

EARLY DAYS

I do not know your age at all, but think that it
    could be,
That you were born before HP or black and white
    T.V.
If that is so those holidays we all now take abroad,
Would be exclusive to the rich, who really could
    afford.
'Hardware' came in tin or brass, there were no
    plastic kits.
And 'Software' would be woollen goods,
    pullovers, gloves, or mitts.
Hovercraft and trimarans, beefburgers and those
    pizzas,
Are modern names for modern times, each having
    modern features.
In days gone by we married first and then together
    lived,
There were no drink dispensers we drank coffee
    that was sieved.
'Gay' people were a carefree lot the party's life
    and soul,
No longer does it mean the same, as this word
    someone stole.
Coke was Coca Cola, and grass grew on our
    lawns,
Aids was help for someone ill or perhaps someone
    who mourns.
Spaceships were pure fiction. James Bond was
    not yet born,

Laurel Hardy and Mae West, were entertainment's
    norm.
Diseases caused through smoking is a proven fact
    to day,
Then smoking was in fashion, now smoking's
    'Where you may'.
Satellites they can't be true, they would have
    caused derision,
Space flights, moonwalks, they all do say, were
    left for 'Men of vision'.
Computer books and Laptops too were not yet on
    the shelf,
Perhaps in fifty years from now, you'll update
    this poem yourself.

INTOLERANCE

I suppose we should apologise,
When we chop a worm in two,
Or kill a creepy crawly,
Or a slug that's bothering you.

I suppose we should apologise,
To creatures great and small,
Who get annihilated,
Just because they live at all.

Why not apply these standards,
To colour, race and creeds,
And just for once apologise,
And accept they too have needs.

Everyone and everything,
Has use on earth today,
It's time we quickly understood,
The importance that they play.

All troubles wane with tolerance,
Try understanding those,
Who seem to us so different,
That some threat to us they pose.

Next time please do apologise,
When you chop a worm in two,
And hope that it reminds you,
There ARE millions NOT LIKE YOU.

THE INSOMNIAC

Tick tock, drip drip, I simply cannot sleep,
The clock's a ticking nuisance, from my window
    I could leap,
Except my home's a bungalow, so I would do no
    damage,
I'd put a hammer through the clock, if I thought I
    could manage.

If not tick tock, then it's drip drip, from my stupid
    water tap,
I have replaced the washer, and the 'S' type
    drainage trap,
I could turn off the water, but I'd have no central
    heat,
Then I would never get to sleep, with frozen icy
    feet.

Cheep chirp, cheep cheep, it's four or five each
    morning,
When all the birds in Christendom, just wake up
    without warning,
But why sit on my roof and fence, producing
    morning tweet,
Just because their tummies need some grubs and
    worms to eat?

Why can't they sleep till ten o'clock, (in a sound
    proof nest, of course)
Or see a Birdie soccer match and tweet until
    they're hoarse?

I really really am fed up, why should they need to
   feed?
They're adamant I'll get no sleep to satisfy my
   need.

I've oiled all locks and hinges too and closed my
   windows tight,
So now there is no change of air, so I can't sleep
   at night.
Oh no! Oh dear, I greatly fear, if I don't get sleep
   soon,
I'll have to take astronomy and contemplate the
   moon.

The hotel's noisy heating system, prompted me to
write this poem. Three nights of purgatory!!

THE LITTLE ONE

With ten little fingers, and ten pinky toes,
Two pretty blue eyes, plus a cute button nose,
You've come to this world and with open eyes,
You find you've a Mummy. What a pleasant
  surprise!

Look after new Mummy and new Daddy too,
You'll soon get them trained, into what's best for
  you.
So go easy at first and don't mention nappy,
For they'll love and feed you and keep you quite
  happy.

Expect the odd pain, the scrape and the fall,
You've no need to worry, with good parents on
  call,
Then later Dad may buy a train set 'for you',
And if you are good, you may play with it too.

LOST INNOCENCE

When I was a young boy of seven or eight
My Daddy had died, Mummy had a new mate,
Sunday mornings I'd sneak into bed between both,
Mum went to the kitchen. He'd snuggle up close,
He'd then hold my hand and say, 'Do as I say,
I'll show you some nice games that we two can play.'
At first pain and guilt would bring tears to my
    eyes,
'Now don't tell a soul or I'll claim it's all lies,
And if you tell mummy she'll blame it on you,
Cos this is our secret, that's just for us two.'
It's our 'game' and we played it again and again,
I'd got used to his actions, but not without pain.
As months turned to years and I grew strong and
    tall,
My step dad had taught me to give him 'My all',
I'd grown up too quickly, all due to his 'Game',
I'd been torn apart by my own guilt and shame.
But as I grew older, I learned it was wrong,
So I sought out my school friend, who's wiser
    and strong,
And this loyal friend told his Mum of my plight,
Step Dad was arrested that very same night.
My counselling's helping, which is a good sign,
My pain, guilt and anguish are his and not mine.
He'd taken my childhood, with his 'grown up
    game',
And though I'll survive it will ne'er be the same.
There's a great many years before that man's
    released,
The longer he serves, the more I'll be pleased.

THE LOON
(THE NORTHERN DIVER IN THE U.K.)

There's a beautiful loon on every lake,
It's a state protected bird,
You'll never forget the calls they make,
From dusk to dawn they're heard.

Each call they make throughout the day,
Means much to every loon,
From 'Go away' to 'She's my mate',
Or 'Please chucks come home soon'.

They dive, they swim and fish all day,
Don't ever interfere,
Or the law will have its legal way,
And the loons may disappear.

Their perilous nesting habitat,
Should never be disturbed,
Each parent on their eggs have sat,
Till the birth of the baby bird.

When water borne, the birds with chicks,
Will swim upon 'their' lake,
When tired, a parent's back they'll seek,
Upon which beds they make.

As grown up birds, they'll fly away,
To one of ten thousand lakes,
They'll claim a lake and find a mate,
And so on – to propagate.

So please don't make these lovely birds,
Fly from 'Their' lakes in fear,
Enjoy their tricks and calls you've heard,
And they'll still be there next year.

Dedicated to all *water born birds, throughout the world each with their own songs.*

THE MARRIAGE CODES

The basis of good marriage is of friendship and
of love,
They both have lots in common, go often hand in
glove,
Never keep those secrets, away from one another,
There is no turning back for you, or running home
to Mother.
You both now have four parents each, and you
must not ignore them,
Don't let them get out of your reach, just love
them and adore them.
Appreciate each other, in every thoughtful way,
Keep arguments and anger and friction all at bay.
So make up any differences long before nightfall,
And don't maintain your anger, that is no good at
all,
So kiss each other and make up and anger will
soon go,
Hold hands and say 'l love you' this helps your
true love grow.
Remember it's important as sure as night meets
day,
To say that 'I do love you' at least once every
day.
One other thing important is that you understand,
That you will never be too old to hold each other's
hand.
A working marriage is no gift and nor is it a right,
It's something you should work at each day and
every night.

When incidents go 'Pear Shaped', no doubt they
    will sometime,
Then be forgiving – read this code – and things
    will turn out fine.

NEW BABY

Oh, what a clever new baby you are,
To pick such a lovely young Mother and Pa,
They've excellent training and love one another,
So quickly adopt THEM as your Daddy and
Mother.
At first let them think that THEY really know
best,
Occasionally putting them both to the test,
A few sleepless nights and nappies quite messed,
With colic, the burps – not to mention the rest.
Will soon test their strengths and their weaknesses
too,
For it's said that's what babies will quite often
do,
Let them play 'BEING PARENTS' for that is
THEIR role,
THEY'LL soon quickly learn that it's YOU in
control.

NOW AND THEN

Computers and technology and the jargon that is used,

Confused my poor old Grandpa – or possibly amused,

A BUS should carry passengers – into and from the town,

And JUMPERS would be knit in wool, perhaps in red or brown,

BIOS was the weighted side of a crown green bowl, he'd say,

Whereas a BYTE upon 'her' ear and he'd have his wicked way.

A RAM, was sheep, all woolly and of the mannish kind,

And PCs may take you to court and sometimes you'd be fined.

CACHES were the prettiest girls, that all the boys desired,

And HARDWARE includes pots and pans your loving wife admired.

MOTHERBOARD, was when she yawned, fed up with trivial patter,

A PACKET had your wages in (or perhaps a private matter).

WEBSITES were old spiders' homes and full of consumed fly,

Where INTERNET, you'd put your fish, for otherwise they'd die.

MICROCHIPS you wouldn't get from the local fish and chip shops,

Grandpa likes his large and fresh and says they
are the tops.
COMPRESSION could be medical, or an engine's
ratio,
If you know what they mean today – please let
my Grandpa know.

Grandpa says 'They can't even speak proper today
and they certainly can't spell!!'

OUTRAGEOUS

Dear Grandpa,

We sent the undertakers to visit you today,
I believe you didn't answer them, perhaps you
were away,
So I thought that I would write to you, and say
that it is time,
That you packed in in this old world and give me
what is mine.

No point in keeping all that cash, investments and
those savings,
You're spending my inheritance, with all your late
night rave-ins.
You've got a Lamborghini, a Porsche and two
Mercedes,
So when am I to get my share? When you've
stopped courting ladies?

I've got a massive overdraft believing you'd soon
peg it,
When burly debt collectors call, I often have to
leg it.
My wife, I really have to say, spends money just
like water,
She hopes to have a windfall soon, after all she is
your daughter.

You know we really cannot wait until you have
decided,

To give us all that lovely cash which so far you've
   denied us.
So hurry up you old skinflint, for all our sakes,
   please snuff it.
We really cannot live like this, in our mansion we
   must rough it.

We can't afford your funeral costs, you stupid old
   buffoon,
We hope that you've prepaid for it, if not then do
   so soon.
For goodness sake please think of us, you're ten
   years over eighty,
It's time you took an arsenic pill, now that
   WOULD help us greatly.

Love and best wishes,

FLU

When I was first born I had thirty long legs,
But my dad he had near forty some,
He taught me to fly up a human's large nose,
Then lodge in their throats just for fun.

'From their nose and their throat, you can get on
     their chest,'
Said my Dad, who knows all about flu.
'And if you get good, with my training you should,
You can make 'em all choke and turn blue.

'If you don't kill them off, but make them quite
     ill,
You can make them sneeze often, you see,
Then they'll make a queer sound and spray you
     around,
So take aim for the next nose that's free.

'The wonderful thing is the names that you're
     called,
Like Asian, Hong Kong and Beijing,
They'll never stop you, they don't know who you
     are,
So go on lad and have your young fling.

'Being a flu germ's a wonderful thing,
You're safe for there's no antidote,
Don't travel in fear, 'cos you mutate, each year,
Just give 'em all Flu lad and gloat.'

OSCAR'S LUCK

First let me explain about Oscar's small brain,
He had brain cells that weren't close together,
Whenever he started a 'DO IT YOURSELF',
All his neighbours ran off hell for leather.

Once Oscar, the bore, rang the bell of our door,
He showed signs of extreme agitation,
'Now where,' he did plead, 'will I find the mains
    key,
To your water supply's termination?'

Said I, 'In my garage – beneath my work bench.'
Oz said, 'I've not got one in mine.'
'Yes Oz, I do know, so let us both go,
And locate yours, I'm sure that there's time.'

As I passed by his window, some water ran down,
From the water pipe Oscar had struck,
A huge jet of spray was cascading that way,
'Poor Oscar,' said I. 'What bad luck.'

A plumber arrived and effected repairs,
Oz only had six days to wait!
But the shelf that he'd planned, for the wall that
    he'd drilled,
Has still not been built in to date.

A critical look at his patio doors,
Convinced Oscar the locks were too weak,

So he purchased two bolts, for the top and the
   bottom,
Then drilled the surround which is teak.

Now I know it's insane, but here once again,
His drill wandered through onto glass,
As the vacuum sucked in with a terrible din,
Shattered panes filled the room with a crash.

Now Oscar's big dream was a T.V. he'd seen,
For his bedroom to view every night,
So he drilled through the wall from inside to out
But the small hole he drilled was too tight.

Then with hammer and chisel he gave it a whack,
And three bricks from the wall fell outside.
Through conservatory glass – and timber sash,
They made holes in the roof six feet wide.

His son who has brains but nowhere to play trains,
As their lounge has restrictions galore,
Made Oscar think 'Loft' for that's what he'd got,
So proceeded upstairs with his saw.

'Those truss things,' said Oz, 'they spread out
   like wings.'
So removed most to form a clear room,
The additional weight from the decking he laid,
Made the ceilings collapse pretty soon.

The Building Inspector, took Oscar to court
And Oz had to pay a huge fine,

The Architect's builders are very concerned,
Will support for his walls be in time?

If you're in our district we advise you 'Keep
Clear',
Just look for the house that Oz wrecked,
If you have to go near, please use caution – with
fear,
Lest Oscar's Bad Luck takes effect.

My apologies to all those Oscars who aspire to
Do It Yourself – and make a good job of things.
Pity you're not all perfect!!

THE PET

The old lady, I'm told, was a year over eighty,
She was in good health but perhaps a bit weighty,
Her pet was a parrot she'd had since her birth,
It gave her great joy with its banter and mirth.

One night fast asleep, in her comforting bed,
Her sleep was disturbed as poor Polly dropped
    dead,
So Jason her grandson, called on her next day,
To learn that poor Polly had just passed away.

'Don't worry,' said Jason, 'We'll get you another,
We'll all club together, me, Dad and my mother.
I'll go into town to that lovely Pet Store
For a new baby parrot, there's a choice there I'm
    sure.'

In the shop he was told, 'There's an African Grey,
But they're very expensive, I really must say.'
'Does he talk or do tricks?' asked Jason politely,
'Of course,' said the storeman. 'All day and twice
    nightly.'

'You'll note on his right leg a ribbon in red,
And that on the left is a blue one instead.'
''What on earth,' did ask Jason, 'are those ribbons
    for?'
'Now that's the surprise,' said the man in the store.

'The Lord's prayer, if you pull the red ribbon,
  he'll say,
But if blue, the Commandments all ten he'll relay.
I take it you'll buy Nan this beautiful bird,
There's no better talker, that you've ever heard.'

So Jason with Polly and sunflower seeds,
Dashed home to his Nanny, to tell of his deeds.
'What a beauty!' said Grandma. 'You'll be
  pleased to hear,
That our vicar is coming, he's such a sweet dear.'

Introduced to the vicar, the parrot did preen,
With ribbons on legs, no such parrot he'd seen.
'If I pull at the red one, what will Polly say?'
'Why, the Lord's prayer' said Nanny, 'Let's kneel
  down and pray.'

'But what, may I ask, if the blue one I pull?'
'Ten Commandments,' said Nanny. 'He'll say
  them in full.'
'And the two both together, if I should do that?'
'Off my perch you will pull me – YOU STUPID
  OLD BAT.'

*O.K. so it's a very old joke, but I could not resist
putting it to rhyme.*

A REMARKABLE FAMILY

We are a wonderful family, we are,
Me Dad's always drunk and so is me Ma.
A lobotomy robbed me poor Grandpa of brains,
Me brother sucks blood, every night from our
    veins.

Me aunty is known as 'Biotics' by most,
No man in the village is safe – so she boasts.
Me sister's quite crazy on our rugby teams,
Each one of 'em's known her at some time it
    seems.

Me grandma is ninety and still going strong,
But a flagon of whisky just don't last her long.
Me uncle's quite clever, or so the cops say,
They hope to release him, from prison some day.

Our rotweiller's rabid and so vicious too,
He uses our bedroom as his favourite loo.
The cat does his woopsies and wees where he
    may,
There is no control in our house, they do say.

I always see double and lose balance some,
But so does my daughter, also my son.
One grandchild has two heads, the other has three,
A remarkable family, I'm sure you'll agree.

*I refuse to state what prompted me to write this
poem and in the case of a family libel action being
brought against me, I deny ever having seen it!!*

THE RIGHT CODE

The 'Income Tax' staff used to work without face,
Then a miracle happened and they now work with
    grace.
There's humans to talk to – not a stuffed shirt in
    sight,
They all help with your taxes, so that it is right.
At last there's 'Real' people, whose advice you
    can ask,
They're not only helpful but relish the task.
They work out your coding and explain what it
    means,
So you understand it and it is what it seems.
They tell you of errors and correct them in time,
But of course if you're stupid you could get a
    fine.
After Government's portion, what's left MUST
    be mine,
That helps get it right for us all every time.

*This is written as an accolade to all those who
work in the Income Tax departments which have
had a considerable shake up in recent years with
excellent results.*

THE SLOB

My wife accused me of being a slob,
And this I do not understand,
I put on my old Army trousers and boots,
With a bright orange shirt and look grand.

With red and white socks, my ensemble's
    complete,
Plus a bright maroon coat from Oxfam,
As sophisticates go I put on a show,
Quite frankly there's no smarter man.

She claims that my manners are shocking to see,
Slurping soup from my bowl, as one should,
I eat peas off my fork, off my knife I eat pork,
And use fingers on custard and pud.

I help in the house and our large garden too,
I also look after our bar,
I will pass her the mower, the drill or the spade,
I don't use them – that's going too far.
There's nothing will please her and that I must
    say,
I never lift up the loo seats,
I leave scum round the bath, that *she* won't
    remove,
It's annoying when left there for weeks.

I do like my beers and I like three or four,
And often I like even more,

With a bladder like mine, I don't make it each
    time,
So I wet both the seat and the floor.

I can't understand why she claims I'm a slob,
She's too neat and tidy I know,
But as for MY manners, I'll burp when I want,
And with one more complaint, she can go.

SMOKING

I am the kid and this is the cig
That I smoke.

I am the man that owns the shop,
That sells the cigs,
To the kids who smoke.

I am the factory,
That makes all the cigs,
To supply to the man to sell
To the kids who smoke.

I am the hoarding,
With claims of low tar,
On T.V. a poster or formula car,
That shows all the 'Ads' for the man who sells
    cigs
To the kids who smoke.

I am the Government,
That rules our land,
That taxes the profits,
Made from the ads,
And the factory and traders and the man who sells
    cigs,
To the kids who smoke.

I am the smoke,
That drifts here and there,
To invade non-smokers with polluted air,

To give them sore throats and the odd cancer scare,
(Some smokers it seems just don't seem to care),
Like the man in the shop who sells all those cigs,
To the kids who smoke.

I am no longer a kid,
And I regret the sad day,
I became so addicted and now have to pay,
For cigs and those taxes I'd like to prevent,
Those Government taxes now being spent,
On the health costs and research because of the
    cigs,
That are sold by the man in the shop,
To those kids WHO STILL SMOKE.

Readers will recognise that the above poem is NOT in my usual style. Whilst on holiday in Perth I noticed an excellent poem by Dianne M. Barry relating to the misuse of alcohol by today's youth, the sentiments and style impressed me. Dianne Barry works for the Fast Forward Group to assist, council and advise youths who need help relating to drugs, smoking alcohol and solvent abuse. It was at one of their offices that I located her poem. The content of this poem is totally different from that of Dianne Barry's but is written in similar style.

THE VOYEUR

A young lady came in and removed her tracksuit,
Then her sweatshirt and pants, until bare,
She entered the shower and turned up the power,
What a beautiful sight, I declare.

Two younger ones entered in pretty swim suits,
Which they peeled off each other, I see.
And when towelled down, they started to clown,
Chasing each other round with great glee.

It's not often you're placed in the shower changing
    rooms,
And discretion's nine tenths of the rules,
For the ladies undress then they clean up their
    mess,
Before going for a dip in the pools.

Then they use those machines to keep fit and trim,
And later strip off for a shower,
They try other's clothes and then powder their
    nose,
I just watch them for hour upon hour.

The wonderful thing is they don't know I'm here,
With four holes to the wall I've been screwed,
I stand five feet tall and hold gear for them all
As a clothes rack, I cannot be moved.

TAKE-A-NOIDS

Did you say 'Goodbye' today,
To your ADENOIDS, which they do say,
Should be removed as soon as poss?
We're sure you will not feel the loss.

Most hospitals are really great,
For others there to sit and wait,
But not for you, dear friend of mine,
We hope you'll soon be feeling fine.

They call them ADD A NOIDS I see,
This seems the wrong way round to me,
For surely they'll take them away,
So call them TAKE A NOIDS today.

Give nurses, doctors and their crew,
A smile, a kiss and a big 'THANKYOU',
Your TAKE A NOIDS, they now have got,
Your health will now improve a lot.

*Written for our Granddaughter when she had her
'Take A Noids' removed in 1997 and is dedicated
to all those children who finish up 'DEVOID OF
NOIDS'.*

UGLY

I was said to be ugly, the day of my birth,
It filled some who saw me, with laughter and
    mirth,
My eyes were too small and too close together,
And the rest of my body was the colour of leather.
I had short stumpy legs and a fat body too,
With a whacking great mouth, with which I could
    chew.
My ears were quite silly, for the size of my head,
So small but effective, or so it was said.
Like every young baby, I could swim like my Dad,
My tail was no bigger than the average lad.
Now some thought me lovely, a beautiful boy,
And to my dear Mum I was her pride and joy.
My reflection seemed right, so why all the fuss?
After all I'm a baby RHIN-OS-OR-US.

THAT'S LIFE

I would snuggle up tightly, well-fed and quite
 warm,
With my close loving parents, from the day I was
 born.
My Mum never boozed or smoked dreaded weeds,
And both, in their turn, took great care of my
 needs.

Now babies, they say, convert food into poo,
With my tummy quite full, I suppose that is true,
As my Dad and my Mum always fed and changed
 me,
I desperately tried to keep dry my nappy.

Aged one I was crawling, and talked guggly goop,
I'd gone off Mum's milk and ate rusks crushed in
 soup,
I'd pull pussy's tail and grabbed handfuls of fur,
And when kitty scratched back, I just didn't care.

Aged four I could cycle on four wheels not two,
I would talk the hind legs off a donkey, that's true.
Mum taught me some sums, and Dad words I
 could spell,
At nursery school teacher said I did well.

Aged eleven I took the national exam,
With momentary feelings like that of a man,
My friends and I often talked of girls and of sex,
Mostly piffle of course, we'd no training or text.

Most teenagers think, 'We can do anything,'
I generally did – What heartache it did bring.
By twenty life often became somewhat blurred,
With late nights, cute girls and the booze that we
    slurped.

I believe when you're thirty and your job's doing
    fine,
You've a wife who wants children – so you answer
    'In time.'
By forty your tummy expands with your chins,
You are flatulent, balding and have the odd flings.

At fifty your doctor's advice is on food,
He confirms high cholesterol and says that's not
    good.
By sixty your prostate's close friend is your loo,
To make matters worse your deafness shows
    through.

Your ingrowing toe nails and arthritic hip,
Show no signs of easing and give constant gyp.
At seventy it's surgery time for your chins,
With collagen added to the facial tuck ins.

At eighty you've dinner at two in the morning,
With lunch around six without it yet dawning,
That the breakfast you ate the evening before,
Had made you quite sick, all over the floor.

By ninety, you're Ga Ga and talk Googly Goop,
Once again, you eat rusks crushed up in your soup.

Incontinence ruins every night – you're unhappy,
'Til the day nurse arrives to change your wet
   nappy.

One hundred's the age when most people have
   gone
But if you now feel you're still fit and quite strong,
It will suddenly dawn and without too much mirth,
All those things you do now – are repeats of your
   birth.

UPSIDE DOWN

We live in a funny old world today, things seem
    the wrong way round,
The dog sits in YOUR easy chair, his feet don't
    touch the ground.
'Fetch me my tea and biccies please, do not just
    sit and stare,
Jump to it lad and if you're good, I'll let You
    groom My hair.'

I'm sure that you'll soon get the point, as you
    quickly realise,
Our world today is full of things we really do
    despise.
These 'Things' are happening every day, defying
    all logistics,
With druggies, thugs and yobs out there who do
    'Things' just for kicks.

A burglar's in your house again, you punch him
    to the floor,
Police arrive and YOU are jailed, YOU get three
    months or more.
The burglar, he gets reprimand, claiming damages
    galore,
Moreover whilst in jail you think, 'What is wrong
    with our Law?'

Our loved one's killed, by young car thieves, some
    idiots call 'Joy Riders',

THEY get suspended sentences, plus many
    sympathisers.
A murder victim's family loses someone close and
    dear,
And sees the murderer stay in jail for less than
    seven year.

There are hundreds of advisers, for those who
    commit crime,
But nothing's done to ease the pain, for the victims
    at this time.
That's why the dog feels quite at ease, to sit in
    YOUR easy chair,
Who is there then to say he's wrong and DOES
    ANYBODY CARE?

Dedicated to Tony

*This poem is dedicated to our nephew, who in
1984 was mowed down by three young car thieves,
who then reversed over him to ensure he was dead.
Eventually identified, after six months of intensive
police investigation, the case was never brought
to Court 'As it was no longer possible to establish
which of the three thugs was driving the vehicle
at that time'!!*

THE CONMAN

I'd read all those books on motor mechanics,
So purchased a tool kit of sockets and 'spanicks',
I forged a good reference and conned my way
    through,
A most pleasant meeting and good interview.

The firm I selected had second hand sales,
They accepted my reference and concocted tales,
'Your wages are boosted by repairs that you make
The more work you "find" the more wages you
    take.'
First came a lady whose car was quite dead,
(She'd run out of petrol), but I simply said,
'Your Hypertorque Thirglib is shattered, that's
    true,
They're very expensive but I'll fit one that's new.'
It was towed round the corner and refilled from
    my tanks,
Then I charged the good lady 'One hundred – with
    thanks.'
My next job went smoothly. A six monthly
    'Routine',
'You're an excellent mechanic I've heard,' said
    Maclean.
'If you find problems, please do not delay,
Whatever you find, should be fixed right away.'
So I 'phoned him to tell him that the Plecsus had
    fused,
And I'd fit him a good one that had been little
    used.

The cost would be modest at two hundred and
  two,
But if he paid cash, then I'd fit one that's new.
Now over the months that I worked for the firm,
I've fitted ten 'Gizmoes' and twelve
  'Snoggletherm'.
Then one day I welcomed Maclean at my door,
'Your repair jobs are rubbish and you'll do no
  more,
I'm a Government Inspector and we've monitored
  you,
As a motor mechanic, you haven't a clue.
However, you'll get ample time when in court,
To answer all charges my department has
  brought.'

So I gave up 'mechanics' and do building instead,
'Cos the householder in general, is more easily
  led.

VIAGRA

A team of British Scientists,
For Pfizer, they do say,
Were set a task to make a pill,
To take heartache away.
They made a pill, they tried it out,
On men who were off guard,
Now on their hearts it did not work,
But their naughty bits got hard.
Pfizer were surprised by this,
But recognised potential,
Replacing all those big soft things,
With things as hard as pencil.
Looking for a powerful name,
They thought of 'Falls Niagara',
But Pfizer wished to raise not fall,
So they called their pill VIAGRA.

Titanic sleeps in Atlantic deep
And is part of history,
The suggestion is to use the pill
To raise this mystery.

An organ appeal at our local church,
Gave the vicar a big surprise,
With Viagra pills to cure his ills,
He now shows his organ with pride.

In Harold's throat the pill stuck fast.
His neck stayed stiff for days,
He sincerely hopes Viagra now,

Is just a passing craze.

Joe took the pill and went up the hill,
To see if he really could,
But a knock on the door,
Brought him downstairs once more,
And there a policewoman stood,
The policewoman said, 'Have I got you from bed,
I need answers if you will agree,
Your wife's lost this locket,
Is that a torch in your pocket,
Or are you just pleased to see me?'

John took Viagra, in Blackpool one night,
The Tower stood upright and bright,
'Please come to bed,' John's wife to him said,
'That Tower will stand there all night.'

Viagra is good, but we really should,
Ask questions and get a reply,
If you're a soft thing and lacking in zing,
Would you on Viagra rely?
American men take the pill now and then
And some even take it each day,
But with heart disease, Viagra may please,
And your life is with what you may pay.

WHO NEEDS YOU

What is religion all about,
It's the cause of many wars,
Why are there many different ones,
Each one with its own laws?

Some mad fanatics are the cause,
With beliefs that they have got,
No use them trying to change the world,
Where you MUST join THEIR lot.

Much better being a Christian,
To help all those in need,
Than wage a war, ignore the poor,
Causing famine, hate and greed.

I don't think I'm religious,
Though I'd do nobody harm,
When others are bereaved or ill,
I'll help them to keep calm.

Perhaps I'm not religious,
Though a Christian I may be,
For I have to help all those I meet,
Less fortunate than me.

It could be why, when in a church,
Tranquillity reigns supreme,
And I think of those less fortunate,
Than I have ever been.

So let's combine religions,
To form one single queue,
To help all those in dire distress,
And those WHO DO NEED YOU.

THE DOCTOR

You have been ill a few times, throughout the year
just gone,
You've visited your doctor and 'waited far too
long',
You've been prescribed some tablets to cure
tummy pranks,
But did you give your doctor a sincere vote of
thanks?
You know the hours that you work by Union
Convention?
Your doctor's done about twice that and that's
without intention.
When Christmas looms up, once again, give
thoughts to doctors too,
For they have family lives to lead, it's really up
to you.
Break nothing over Christmas, it's your doctor
who needs breaks,
Don't drink too much or over eat for everybody's
sake.
Just get some Alka Seltzer or Ant acids that you
chew,
For tummy aches or head pains, they may just
cure you.
Let's give them all a well-earned rest, for all their
families' sakes,
Unless you're Really Really ill, please let them
have their breaks,
It means they'll have their Christmas pud with
family in their home,

So carefully ASSESS YOURSELF before you
   touch that 'phone.

TUM TUM TUM

I was pink and happy and a long wriggly worm,
And lived in the garden at Joe's
I'd wiggle and wriggle converting his plot,
Into superfine soil – as one knows.
One day whilst I sunbathed somewhere near Joe's
   lake,
A starling caught sight of my head.
I couldn't escape and got caught in his grasp,
And he swallowed me whole – but not dead.

Inside of the starling's great rumbling tum,
I frankly could not see a thing,
But faintly I heard the big tom cat next door,
As at bird catching cat Tom was king.
So he then stalked 'Mine Host' with such
   wonderful skill,
And pounced before birdie could fly,
Then two minutes later, the bird filled Tom's tum,
In a tum – In a Tom, there was I!

Now what a position, I thought to myself,
As Joe's dog also entered the fray,
He 'dropped' poor puss cat with one vicious blow,
Then devoured poor Tom the next day.
Now the problem was worse and somewhat
   perverse,
As the tums I was in were now three.
As inside a dog was a cat and a bird,
How on earth could I ever get free?

Good fortune abounded with fate on my side,
Joe's woof dog decided to stray,
Across the main road where the traffic was brisk,
The poor doggie got killed the same day.
Joe buried his pet in the garden we'd dug
With Joe's spade and of course help from me,
It wasn't too long, I made holes in three tums,
Tum Tum Rumbly Tum – 'Now I'm free'.

OUR WISH

When Christmas bells are ringing, in happiness
    and mirth,
And all our choirs are singing to wish us peace
    on earth,
Each heart is overflowing, with greetings warm
    and true,
A time for celebration and confirm their love for
    you.

They'll wish you health and happiness throughout
    the coming years,
That you relax at Christmas time, as another year
    appears,
That your love for all of those you love, will never
    ever waiver,
And life is very good to you and grants for you
    this favour.

AFTER LIFE

If in Heaven you're chosen, then please under-
    stand,
For miniaturisation, the Japs are on hand.
If it's huge and quite costly, the Americans are
    keen,
And for organisation the German's supreme.
With mechanical problems or structural design
The Scots lads are here, their solutions are fine.
The cooks are all French, their cuisine is so good,
And all the good lovers are Spanish by blood.
As for cars or the motor bike driven at speed,
Mediterranean Italians are all that you need.
If it's safety at work and rules by 'The Book',
Go to Britons in Heaven, you've no further to
    look
But with profits and money, you could do much
    worse,
Than go to the Swiss, who hold the world's purse.

If it's Hell that is calling for you to go to,
The pork butchery's run by a Rabbi or two,
Miniaturisation would be left to 'The Yanks',
The Scots put their money in their sporran's not
    banks,
Japanese lovers are the first in the queue,
As for Swiss racing drivers there are but a few.
For the French the odd strike is not to the book,
All main meals when in Spain contain oil as they
    cook,

Your life style decides on which group you will
    join,
For I'm sure it's not left to the toss of a coin.

DEMISE

The chaps in your company are very disturbed,
By your serious illness, they also have heard,
That the Governor's dying and there is no cure,
We cannot conceive how your loss we'll endure.
We've had a collection for flowers and beer,
There's no need to worry, the coffin is here,
Too bad, we can't cheer you in your last hours,
Remember the proverb, 'We'll say it with
    flowers'.

The coffin we made up of angle and plate,
Caused your funeral party to run a bit late,
The stairs were the problem, a real awkward set,
Your manager stated, the most awkward he'd met.
We dismantled your sidewall and the stairs in the
    hall,
But no need to dismantle the front garden wall,
With jumbo and derrick plus burners and tackle,
We soon got the work done, without further
    prattle.

Now that you've left us, you missed all of the
    fun,
Four million, just over, on the Lottery we've won,
Just two days had gone and the grass seed was
    sown,
But we've one consolation, our profits had grown.
It is such a pity – you were such a nice fellow,
But never relaxed, except on your pillow.

REPLIES

So now, at last, the whole truth is out,
Your Governor's 'The man' when passing out,
The cost of the flowers and bitter beer,
You all collected with so much good cheer.
But just wait, you wishful scheming bods,
I'll not lie quietly 'neath all these sods.
For whilst you thought that I was expiring,
I've also completed my own conspiring.
I've conjured up a most drastic scheme,
For forcing you lot to work as a team.
I'll break your hearts in such a way,
That you'll still work hard for your minuscule
     pay.
So bow down your heads in shameful grief,
What! Plates and scrap angle for your old Chief?
Nay! good polished oak and chromium plate,
Clearly engraved with name, rank and date.
The National Lottery that you thought you'd won?
Well the bets I just kept and I did not place one,
But banked all the 'loot' in the name of my wife,
So get back to work for the rest of YOUR life.

BE POSITIVE

You may think that there is no cure,
For the illness of you or your friend,
But with research and technical study,
Our scientists will fight to the end.

So it's best not to look round the corners,
Into alleyways that seem so grim,
Take courage and look far beyond them,
And research must surely win.

A WEIGHTY PROBLEM

As I lay on the floor, I could look up her skirt,
Oh dear! What a sight I did see,
There were great rolls of fat on her huge calves
    and thighs,
In an instant I knew she'd hurt me.

As she raised her left foot the floor gave a groan,
Then she placed her huge leg near my face,
She followed this up with her right leg – as large,
And my strain gauge near snapped out of place.

She couldn't care less, as I sank to the floor,
'You're twenty-eight stone,' I did state,
'Don't be stupid,' she said, 'that just cannot be,
You're suggesting that I'M overweight?'

My job is too stressful with such folk around,
I just wish they were more slim and lean,
I've a terrible job as I am so abused,
That's the life of a weighing machine.

MILLENNIUM

When we first started counting our years in A.D.
It was called year ONE as we changed from B.C.
And with no more numerals to come in between,
When is our Millennium, or has it just been?

By adding two thousand to year ONE A.D.
Two thousand and one, is the year that I see.
Dionysius' nickname was one 'Doggy Knees'!
Said Millennium is year '99, if you please.

Whilst Gospels state Herod gave orders to
    slaughter,
The first born of everyone's son or a daughter,
But Herod did die at least four years B.C.
Which means Jesus Christ was born five years
    'pre'.

That puts the millennium nineteen ninety-six,
Which leaves us a mess that I hope we can fix.
Julius Caesar said, 'Years have three fifty-four
    days,
But add a few in, only when I do says.'

An Egyptian advisor said, 'Caesar, you're wrong,
There's three sixty-five and each fourth you add
    one.'
So now you will see we were still in a mess,
Till our Roger Bacon declared, 'But it's less.'
As three sixty-five and one quarter day,
Is eleven mins too long in each year, he did say,

In October of year fifteen eighty-two,
They added ten days, to get out of their stew.
Since then all these minutes did simply accrue,
When is the Millennium? I wish that I knew.

NEW YEAR

When his young son awoke, he was very upset,
He'd been diddled out of a full year,
For he went to bed in the year ninety-eight,
Sleeping soundly 'til morning was near.

But when he awoke, the poor little bloke,
Found the year was then ninety-nine,
Said the lad with a whine 'Eight from a nine?
Where's my year gone in such a short time?'

No wonder the lad was so very upset,
He thought that he'd slept through a year,
'Never mind,' said his dad, 'I'm sure you'll be
    glad,
You've a birthday again this New Year.'

WORLDLY

Our earth as a planet, viewed from outer space,
Is a colourful, beautiful, wonderful place,
The sun provides heat through our own
  atmosphere,
And the ozone prevents heat reflecting from here.

It seems that we've all signed a suicide pact,
As we destroy our planet – a well proven fact.
We belch out pollution from cars, gas and coal,
Ignoring reductions, we've set as our goal.

Global warming's increased so the ice starts to
  melt,
And even today, the result's being felt,
With tornadoes and flooding and water still rising,
Such a change in the weather, should not be
  surprising.

So the water continues to rise at a pace,
There's few taking action at this threat to our race,
We still landfill bottles, tins, cardboard and paper,
How long will we proceed with this stupid caper?

Recycling would help, plus more house insulation,
To progress recycling we need plant installation,
Use of bikes, public transport, car share and to
  walk,
Should all now be actioned and with far less talk.

So turn off that light, turn the thermostat low,
Draught proof the house, double glaze as we go.
Control works' discharges and farming 'By
    spray',
Let's all get involved. WE MAY YET SAVE THE
    DAY'.

R.I.P.

My first wife was a nagger, but had plenty of cash,
She 'jumped' in the river and made quite a splash,
Police never found who tied rope round her leg,
Or put all that concrete in the old beer keg.
My second was taking a bath late one night,
A shock from the fire killed the poor girl outright,
I'd tested the cable length, one day before,
From inside the bath to the plug near the door.

My third wife, they thought, had tripped over the cat,
I disposed of all labels which said paraquat,
She took deadly poison through a small rubber hose,
With the help of a clip found attached to her nose.
My fourth wife was active but unfit and quite plump,
She insisted on trying her first bungee jump,
I'd measured the rubber in metres not feet,
But it should have been yards, so her head hit the street.

My fifth wife was killed whilst driving her car,
The brake system failed, so it travelled too far,
The hydraulic pipes had been severed right through,
I disposed of my hacksaw the moment I knew.
My sixth wife quite suddenly took her own life,
A terrible shock as she used a long knife,

She stabbed herself twice, in the back, with hands
    tied.
It showed how determined she was to have died.

I changed their Insurance each time that I claimed,
No sinister motives, I just hate to get blamed,
In each case they paid me a very large sum,
And each wife I lost, enhanced my income.
My last wife was pretty and knew I was wealthy,
I'd flu at the time and did not feel too healthy,
She got medication from a close 'friend' she knew,
I've taken a dose. She says arsenic cures flu!!.

T.V.

That annoying television is blurting out again,
At this time in the morning, it really is insane,
I told the kids the night before, the T.V.'s out of
   bounds,
I'm fed up with the stupid progs and aggravating
   sounds.
O.K. I thought, ten times I've caught
Them viewing early mornings,
So I went and switched the power off,
For ignoring all my warnings.
Without mains power, the house alarm,
Sprang into loud response,
Neighbours quickly phoned police who also came
   at once.
The cat and dog from number nine, decided it
   was time,
To have a fight and then take fright,
And up the tree did climb.
The escalating problems, put the Fire Brigade on
   call,
But as they raised a ladder, pussy fell and hit a
   wall.
The dog raised Cain by barking and ran into the
   road,
The Medic's car arrived just then and down the
   dog he mowed.
Home Watch neighbours weren't too pleased,
For causing all the fuss,
So far they'd lost a good night's sleep,
One dog and one black puss.

Meanwhile power had been restored,
And the tele was switched on,
I went outside and found a brick,
They'll not watch that for long.

Dedicated to our grandson, Daniel, but don't ask why!

MUMMY'S BOY

Mum was distraught as her son, so she thought,
Could manage quite well on his own,
So she made out a list, gave the lad a big kiss,
And said, 'Off to the shop – and don't moan.'

So the lad went outside, then suddenly cried,
'Hey Mam, I can't open the gate.'
'Then you'll just have to learn, there's the handle
   you turn,
So be gone and please don't be late.'

He went through the gate and returned in a state,
'Mam, I'm lost when I venture outside,
Can't I play with my toys, I won't make a noise?'
'Oh grow up lad,' his mother replied.

She was somewhat surprised at the short steps he
   took,
Then she noticed his shoes gave him bother,
Each shoe had a bow, but the daft so and so,
Had tied both his shoestrings together.

As she knelt on the floor she noticed he wore,
His trousers were on front to back,
So she undid his laces and also his braces,
And gave his bare bottom a smack.

'Now empty your pockets, get a clean hanky too,
What's this, marbles, some string and something
   you chew,

One penknife, four labels, two stamps, which look
    new,
For goodness sake lad – what am I to do?'

Quite frankly she thought, she'd already taught,
Her son not to dress in that state,
She was obviously wrong, saying, 'Come on now
    son,
After all, you are twenty-eight!'

HUBBY

His dear loving spouse, asked for help round the
    house,
Being pregnant and soon due to whelp,
If I do this week's wash and the ironing as well,
Then I'm sure that will be a great help.

So he put all the clothes in the washing machine,
With a cup full of powder he'd seen,
They then splish splashed an hour and spin dried
    a while,
He was proud of the great help he'd been.

When he opened the door, most clothes fell on
    the floor,
So he dumped them all into the sink,
There were skirts, vests and blouses and one pair
    of trousers,
But the lot were a delicate pink.

Now that's funny he thought, that white shirt that
    I bought,
Is now pink – there is something not right,
Why is there no book, to tell you to look,
And wash coloureds quite separate from whites?

Then he opened the door of the hot air machine
And bundled the yucky mess in,
Something strange caught his eye, a black flash
    passing by,
His puss cat was in a fast spin.

This shock to the wife, made him call the midwife,
But too late came a cry from the floor,
Pink clothes, one crushed puss and a babe in a
    rush,
She showed her dear husband the door.

ZOLL

Zoll was instructed to go down to earth,
To establish if life forms existed,
You'll get bus number three, there's a seat that is
    free,
Controlling Space Council insisted.

So he waited an hour for the number three bus,
Then four arrived all out of turn,
Zoll said, 'You're late.' 'So what – you can wait,'
Said the driver who showed no concern.

The Cosmonaut driver – a green man from Mars,
Had four eyes and two horns on two faces,
With feet to the floorboards, they hit hyperspace,
To find out about Earth's human races.

They landed near cones by a great pile of stones,
That were upright, with some on the top,
Zoll, thought of the life form he may find on Earth,
Will his mission result in a flop?

So thinking who's who and what do they do?
Have they two legs, or four, with a tail?
Do they speak? Are they short, are they fat, do
    they squeak?
Are they female or are they all male?

He'd not long to wait to resolve his debate,
What appeared had long floppy ears,
They all looked around but made not a sound,

They had white fluffy tails at their rears.

Then landing near by, black things from the sky,
With long yellow points on their faces,
He heard nought but tweets, as they grabbed
    worms to eat,
Then flew off on two wings without traces.

A third group arrived, with strange things on their
    heads,
And a thin twitching tail at the rear,
Zoll talked to them all, but they bleated a call,
Then suddenly dashed off in great fear.

So back he did climb, to his Spacebus on time,
Just as Space Centre ordered 'All Clear'.
To his Council, he brought his discerning report,
About rabbits and birds and some deer.

So when space ships arrive, please don't go and
    hide,
It confuses our neighbours in space,
Be proud that we're 'Man', converse all we can,
And progress in this technical race.

Drawing hasty conclusions when he thought that
    'He knew',
Is something we all tend to do,
Don't take all YOU'VE heard, however absurd,
Or conclusions you draw won't be true.

SCHOOL

Miss Pringle, our teacher, with blackboard and
    chalk,
Wrote down several numbers then gave us a talk,
'There's a two and a two and one nine twenty-
    two,
'That's the date for today, I suppose you all knew?

'Now what time will elapse when each two
    becomes three?
And no shouting out, put your hands up for me.'
''Leven-year,' said our know-all, the horrible lad,
It was 'Old Smelly Smithers' he made us so mad.

Later his head was stuffed down the boys' loo,
All the girls on the playground were invited too,
Why do all school show-offs give answers galore,
And the rest have no answers, as their maths are
    so poor?

Geography being the afternoon's lesson,
She said, 'It's New Zealand – in our very next
    session,'
'Done it,' said Smelly, once again on the ball,
His correct snappy answers embarrassed us all.

Miss Pringle said, 'Plus the three R's that you
    learn,
All curriculum subjects should be your concern.
Some of you're wasting your time at my school,
Concentrate on your lessons, stop playing the
    fool.'

I meet Cabbage and Toby and his brother called
    Freak
At the Local Job Centre every Thursday, each
    week,
We agree on one thing, Pretty Pringle was right,
If we'd listened to her we'd not be in this plight.

Smithers of course, is not longer called Smelly,
He's a very important presenter on 'Tele',
And is making a programme 'Education and
    Schools',
It includes all the 'Toby's' and similar fools.

WORDS

Words are so important,
And also how they're said,
When not expressed correctly,
You may finish up misled.
Some carry great importance,
Far beyond their size,
'I must admit that I was wrong,'
Must surely take first prize.
'You've really done a first class job,'
Will also take some beating,
And, 'What is your opinion?'
Shows viewpoints that are meeting.
'If you please' and 'Thanks so much',
Will indicate respect,
That's something everyone must earn
And simply not expect.
But 'I' is one more little word,
The smallest of them all,
That is the LEAST important one
That people should recall.

TRAINS

Gone are the days when a train had steam engines
and crew,

It would run down the track with a 'clickerty
click',

Then suddenly whistle 'Choo Choo'.

As you sat in the carriage, it would rock to and
fro,

And sometimes would sway to both sides,

When you opened a window, the smoke billowed
in,

And you'd often get soot in both eyes.

When it passed over points, the rhythmic click
click,

Would change to a clackerty clack,

As the points had been cleared it progressed down
the track,

And the clickerty click would come back.

In a corridor train, for a drink or a snack,

You'd keep a tight grip on each side.

You'd find that the bacon was greasy and cold

And the bread's curly edges had dried.

In the restaurant, you'd get a far poorer deal,

With burnt bangers and mash and stewed tea,

As you'd struggled this far, you would search for
the bar,

To find beers that were warm and cloudy.

If their wine was as cold as the buffet's main
course,

And their meal was as hot as their wine,

If their soup was as thick as the custard they
    served,
Then be sure it was not served on time.
When at a station the train makes a stop,
You'd look at the clock – You are late,
You drop to the platform, collectors await,
To take tickets and check on their date.
If you'd fiddled a ride, he'd say 'Please step
    aside.'
There'd be traffic police at your side,
But with modern trains, there's no losses, all gains.
With good food and those smooth silent rides.

BUSES

George was a driver of double deck buses,
He'd a weird sense of humour, he enjoyed evening
   rushes,
A crowd at a bus stop, where they ought to wait,
Caused a twitchy right foot and he'd accelerate.

Any dear lady with zimmer support,
Would cause George to stop to continue his sport,
For just as she placed her zimmer on board,
George's foot would slam down and off his bus
   roared.

His best moments came when school children
   went home,
For he'd scatter the lot every which way that's
   known,
The lads at his depot said he was perverse,
If you dare stop behind him, he'd be sure to
   reverse.

George approached traffic lights with such great
   panache,
He would slam on his brakes, he enjoyed a good
   crash,
With passengers standing, he would brake even
   more,
They would run, trip and stumble to a heap on
   the floor.

Personnel were alerted to his skilled history,

They sent off his file for his depot to see,
The took George off driving, his firm is no fool.
He's now Chief Instructor at their driving school.

TESTING TIMES

I've been testing 'L' drivers on main roads every
    day,
My adrenalin rises when we both drive away,
We have 'Feet to the floorboards in first or
    reverse',
Or others who're so slow, you'd think them
    perverse.
Some red lights mean nothing as through them
    they barge,
My pacemaker's battery needs a mains super-
    charge.
Mr Brown came to town, to achieve his ambition,
But I had to fail him, he couldn't find the ignition.
Miss Jones was my next, she was almost
    undressed,
A pretty young thing, really keen for her test,
I asked her politely, 'Do you use M.S.M.?'
'Of course' she replied, 'I buy most things from
    them.'
'No – no,' I explained, 'Mirror – Signal –
    Manoeuvre,'
'Silly Billy,' she said, 'I'm too fast a mover.'
I asked, 'In the country – name a sign that you'd
    see.'
'Why – Free Ranging Eggs and a Car Park that's
    free.'
'And what else,' I did ask, 'to do with your test?'
'That's simple,' she said, 'Cut flowers – they're
    the best.'
I made no impression on this lady of leisure,

So I changed the subject, to give her good
    measure,
'What's that red circle mean, with a 50 inside?'
'That's your minimum speed on this road,' she
    replied.
'There's a hill coming up. What gear's best for
    you?'
'Oh – my pink mini skirt and this blouse you see
    through.'
I was not getting far with the test in her car,
I'd asked twenty questions – not one right so far.
Meandering back home at some speed over eighty,
With one hand on my knee, I refused to get matey.
Missing cycles, some trucks, two cars and a bus,
She mowed down two dogs and a black and white
    puss.
'Have I passed,' she did ask, 'for I surely drive
    well?'
'You're joking,' I said, 'Is it that hard to tell?
But tell me what tests have you taken to date?'
'I think,' she replied, 'Thirty-seven – or eight.'
'Thirty-nine now,' I said, 'But please wait a while,
Before your next test I'm retiring in style.'

BEN

Whilst in his bath young Ben fell asleep,
He had a long think and he thunk,
If I sleep in my bath is the water too deep?
Is it safer to sleep in my bunk?

So from his deep bath he went straight to his bed,
Then he thunked up another big think,
'If I'd stayed in my bath is it warmer instead,
And I'd probably float and not sink.'

So Ben, to his bath, he climbed in once again,
And found out that the water was cold.
Mum said, 'Now then Ben, off to bed you must
    go
Will you please simply do as you're told.'

Ben's 'jamas, of course, were soaking wet
    through,
He'd forgotten to take the things off,
So his bunk got a soak as he lay there all night,
Now Ben thunks he's developed a cough.

But worse was to come as in came his Mum,
And found that his bed was wet through,
'For goodness sake, Ben, do you still not know
    when,
It is way past your time for the loo?'

DRUGS

Do you remember the old nursery rhyme 'This old man'? It started Nick Nack Paddywack give a dog a bone. Well clear your larynx and get into tune for:

Mick Slack 'n Paddy Wack,
Said 'Keep drug dogs at home,
Customs man please do not phone.'

Customs man, he had one.
He found Smack within their 'drum',
With a Mick Slack 'n paddy Wack,
He showed his dog their home,
Smackhead Mick had quickly flown.

Customs man, he knew too,
He'd find Smack in Jack's old shoe,
So with Mick Slack 'n Paddy Wack,
They let the drugs dog roam,
Customs drug haul it had grown.

Customs man, with all three,
They got down upon one knee,
So with Mick Slack 'n Paddy Wack,
They searched for heroin,
Customs man knew that he'd win.

Customs man, on all fours,
He found needles by the score,
So with Mick Slack 'n Paddy Wack,

Plus Whizz and speed galore,
Arrests were quickly made by law.

Customs man, home at five,
Thankful to have left their 'dive',
Now as Mick Slack 'n Paddy Wack
Are safely in their cell,
There's not much more that we can tell.

EFELUMP

There are wonderful aminals called Efelumps,
They have flipperty flopperty trunks in their
    fronts,
They have wiggerly woggerly tails at their rears,
But what of their great flopping flapperty ears?
The Efelumps from Africa's ears are gynormous,
Whilst Indian cousins are not so enormous.
It takes twenty-three months before baby arrives,
So with all that time, it's no great surprise,
Mummy-to-be will get help from them all,
When the big day arrives – do they make a trunk
    call?

FRUSTRATED

I have shopped at this store for ten years or more,
And I knew where each product was placed,
In the very first aisle there were clothes – modern
style,
In aisle two, there were wines – some were cased.

There was meat in aisle three, fillet, sirloin and
tee,
And just opposite – fishes galore,
But then came our loss, as they got a new boss,
Now you can't find a thing anymore.

The meat counter's been moved and they say it's
improved,
And that customers like to search round,
But the 'powers that be' do not seem to see,
Our frustration if products aren't found.

In our superstore it's no fun anymore,
Unsliced bread is three aisles from the cutters,
Long life UHT is still where it should be,
But fresh milk has been moved next to butters.

They no longer provide, or perhaps they just hide,
Many products we used to enjoy,
They say it's to sell their own lines which sell
well,
The whole thing is a Headquarters ploy.

We've talked to the manager, two or three times,

He can't change any Headquarters's scheme,
Well we've news for the store, we won't enter
   their door.
Till goods stay where they always have been.

GOLFS

Whilst driving down the road one day,
There was a signpost, which did say,
'Golf Driving Range – next on the right,'
I did not know Golfs were so bright.

They really must have hearts of steel,
To get behind a steering wheel,
Not on main roads – their skills are poor,
So they need a practice range I'm sure.

HAGGIS

We arrived in the land of the Haggis in May,
Or was it in June or July?
As we entered their Homeland somewhere in the
hills,
A huge billboard lay by a lay-by.

It said 'Buy haggis here, supplied with a beer,
And served with hot tatties and neaps,
We respect haggis breeds, they're protected by
deed,
And we never shoot them as they sleep.'

There were thousands of haggis at play on the
hills,
Some scampering round on the ground,
Whilst others were practising their special skills,
Like the group that we saw flying round.

But the haggis, poor thing, goes in fear every
spring,
It's the main hunting season we heard,
Which goes on for six months, till September
comes,
Then the 'Haggis Protection's' observed.

They free range from September to early
December,
Some time, late in May, babes are born,
They're a wee fluffy beasty, their pink nose match
their feetsy,

They are black, white or brown – some are fawn.

Now haggis demand more respect than they get,
There's many a Scot keep a pair as their pet,
When well fed and watered, they breed twice a
    year,
No wonder there's thousands of haggis round
    here.

HOISTED

On the site where George worked the lads never
    shirked,
But this day their Gaffer looked worried,
'Please be on your guard and work very hard,
Be methodical, neat and unhurried.'

'The building Inspector and our own Director,
Are to visit around ten o'clock,
There's a full site inspection, it's for your
    protection,
So they'll visit the whole building block.'

George, on fifth floor, saw them starting their tour,
The inspector said, 'Let's test your hoists,
They're often the cause for concern due to flaws,
In the pulleys the sheaves or the joists.'

'Send down the contraption I'll study its action,'
George rightly complied on command.
He released his large skip, which was set 'Auto-
    Tip',
And it hurtled to earth full of sand.

The Inspector stood by as the skip flashed on by,
And buried in sand, the Director,
It came to a stop and then landed on top,
Of the poor unsuspecting Inspector.

As it snapped to a close it then suddenly rose,
With the Building Inspector 'In situ',

Whilst still afloat, he got pen, pad and wrote,
'Repairs to the hoist – overdue.'

George was upset, when he knew he would get,
The Inspector upon 'his' fifth floor,
So he thought, 'What a wheeze, if I pull the release
He will plummet once more to the floor.'

His Director, upset, had managed to get,
Extricated from ten tons of sand,
Just in time, it appears, as the skip reappears,
Plus Inspector with pad in his hand.

It seemed no one worried to be in a hurry,
To dig out the Inspector from sand,
For underneath him, was another, now thin,
Ex-Director, which was far from planned.

'Now look here lad, it isn't all bad,
No one knows that on site they have called -
Fill the hole up 'dead neat', flush off with
    concrete,
And George – get the damned hoist overhauled.'

MABEL

My dear Auntie Mabel, some say is unstable,
As she loves to jump out of air planes,
But not with a chute – no nothing so cute,
Just a bungee chord, tied to her reins.

She goes to the door, bungee tied to the floor,
And launches straight off with great glee,
As she plummets to earth, she giggles with mirth,
Her utter delight's plain to see.

Unlike me and you that's not all that she'll do,
She's a kite which she flies under water,
She arm wrestles with crocs, unloads ships at the
    docks,
And at poker, she 'takes lambs to slaughter'.

She loves wild tiger stalking and high wire
    walking,
And in waters infested by sharks,
She will hire a boat, mono ski and a float,
And go for a slalom for larks,

She's a healthy sex life but is nobody's wife,
You're not safe if you're male, in good health,
She makes the advance, if you dare give a glance.
Then look out, she'll use cunning and stealth.

My dear Auntie Mabel is perfectly stable,
Like her friends she will not vegetate,
So if you're a good sport, to Mabel report,
And at last you may find your soul mate.

MOTORING

White lines, yellow lines, some act as if there's
none,
It doesn't matter where they are, they just ignore
each one,
Ignoring limits on our speed of seventy down to
thirty,
Invites a summons with a fine. The driver then
gets 'shirty'.

Excuses range from 'pregnant wives' to 'orders
lost if late',
The driver then expects police to enter in debate,
Police in general are polite and laughing up their
sleeve,
They've heard these stories all before, not one do
they believe.

Three lanes to two or two to one, give drivers
every chance,
There's some will never form a queue, but
stubbornly advance.
Some drive too long on motorways and fall into a
daze,
Whilst others sleep still at the wheel. One question
this does raise,

Should not retraining be made law? Improvements
would be made,
Perhaps we all should just make sure our driving
laws obeyed.

For those of you who think police are persecuting
  you,
Just follow driving laws each trip and the law
  won't bother you.

MUGWOP

I was born very young as a black and white pup,
Most things were a game, that I'd never give up,
In the country we lived on a very large farm,
They had chickens and sheep and some geese in
  their barn.
One day farmer Giles said, 'You'll work for your
  living,
Now listen to me, and instructions I'm giving.'
We all went a walk with my mum up the hill,
Giles blew a small whistle quite strongly and
  shrill,
My mum disappeared up the hill out of sight,
As the sheep reappeared down the hill in full
  flight.
'Oh boy,' I did think, 'This is sure to be fun,'
So I bit at their ankles and the odd woolly bum.
'You daft dog,' said Giles, 'get straight back to
  the farm,
And round up the geese, where you can't do much
  harm.'
So I jumped through the window to where the
  geese were,
Just waiting for round up, and fun, I declare.
Things weren't quite so simple, Mum never
  warned me,
It's the geese do the chasing and I had to flee.
'Let that be a lesson,' said Giles quite upset,
'You're a sheepdog, you Mugwop, not just a house
  pet.'

I spat out goose feathers and a ball of sheep's
    wool,
Now I'm learning my trade and my life's never
    dull.

OLOGY

Henry had tests for a rare allergy,
The main fault was through iodine,
If injected or swallowed the medics would rush,
Or poor Henry became a 'Has Been'.

Fish and chips, tasty crisps, or salt from a pot,
With the smallest wee trace of the stuff,
Would turn his face red, plus his arms and his
    head,
Then his heart and his brain said 'Enough'.

With his doctors' support they recorded his name,
So he carried a disc on his wrist,
'I'll ring up my Mother and likewise my brother,
To tell them my life is at risk.'

So he picked up the phone and found them at
    home,
He said, 'Mum I've a food allergy',
'That's good,' said his Mum, 'so when can you
    come,
With certificates for us to see?

'I always did say that your studies would pay,
And you'd get a real good 'Ology',
So it's food that you've studied as your discipline,
You've made us so proud young Henry.'

'Come, come now,' said Henry to his very proud
    Mum.

'It's not a good food 'Ology'
It's a life threatening thing that iodine will bring.
Get a hearing aid or dic-tion-ary.'

When he went for his dinner the very next day,
He had salty roast beef and a pud.
His brother's broad grin should have warned him
    of sin,
Now Mum's money's his brothers for good.

ONE WAY

Racing down the hill one day,
Moe saw a sign which said 'ONE WAY',
Its arrow pointed to the right,
This gave poor Moe a rotten fright.

He did not know his right from wrong,
So he turned left and flew along,
He heard a 'Poo Parr,' from afar,
And recognised the speeding car.

Blue lamps alight and headlights bright,
Moe hit its bonnet in full flight,
The driver's face had turned bright red,
For he was sure that Moe was dead.

With Moe, on bonnet, sitting still,
Police turned right and up the hill,
Moe thought, 'For goodness sake what next?
They've brought me right back to my nest.'

Book making on that day was brisk,
The odds, of course, reflecting risk,
The village pigeon race each year,
Alerted folks from far and near.

Blue lamps and sirens at full blast,
Made sure the 'boys in blue' weren't last,
The favourite for this year was Moe,
But how on earth were they to know?

They placed their bets, yes every pound,
And lost the lot when they all found,
Their speeding car had stopped Moe's flight,
Because Moe can't tell left from right.

POLITICS

Politicians when in they're in opposition,
Will promise the world without doubt,
But when voted in their whole world turns around,
And their promises then get thrown out.

For instance in year '48, from the State,
It was 'Care for all – cradle to grave',
But when old and infirm needing nursing long
    term,
It's goodbye to life's savings they wave.

However if noses or more private parts,
Need reducing or sometimes made larger,
Make the cliché excuse 'but I'm so traumatised',
And the job is done free, they won't charge yer.

It no longer matters if life is at risk,
Take Viagra and baby creations,
There is some distress, of that there's no doubt,
But why should those costs be our Nation's?

Politicians, meantime, mainly feather their nests,
You would think it was they *who elect us,*
Their salaries are good, but their perks are
    obscene,
With paid seats on some board of directors.

When is it the turn of old folks in our land,
Who had paid more in taxes all round,

And where would the money be found for such
    schemes?
From the Lottery it all should be found.

We've currently paid for a huge stack of tyres,
Plus a pile of old bricks they call art,
But their latest creation from elephant dung,
Was a great waste of wealth from the start.

It's up to M.P.s to change all the rules,
To allow this vast wealth to be used,
The concern of us all is our own Nation's health,
And the income from sales being abused.

RAPE

It was not until I heard of 'The Tape',
I found out that I was accused of her rape,
Her mother and father had no time for her,
But I really did love her and showed her great
    care.

She would snuggle up nightly and hold my hand
    tight,
I'd tuck her in bed and then kiss her goodnight.
She had not developed a feminine chest,
We quite often wrestled, when both fully dressed.

We would romp and had races and had childish
    fun,
And never suspected the great shock to come,
It was four years later, she was then quite mature,
Her home still lacked love and was most insecure.

Of course I'd not seen her throughout those long
    years,
'The tape' which destroyed me confirmed my
    worst fears.
Police did their duty and with great panache,
They were thoughtful and honest, what more
    could I ask.

Her sexual interests, police certified,
That a number of youths had lain down by her
    side,
And once having started to play grown up games

She thought that her father would demand the
　　youths' names.

So she said, 'It's your brother – you won't report
　　me,'
'Oh no,' said her father. 'Then just wait and see.'
The police, the report and the tape are all known,
My response made them think, so they looked
　　'close to home'.

She repented, admitting the tape was all lies,
Now I no longer love her, but do I despise?
The trauma and worry destroyed family pride,
I will never forgive her though I've often tried.

Paedophiles and those who rape – in particular
young children deserve long prison sentences. The
child's trauma must be horrendous. But for those
few innocent men who are erroneously accused,
then their trauma must also be as great, for surely,
they too have been raped?

SIGNS

The workmen had finished their toilet
    construction,
'WET PAINT' said the sign 'this is NOT an
    instruction.'
'CUSTOMER ORDERING POINT' said one
    sign,
They ordered ten thousand, now the store's doing
    fine.
Their blending machine, in the canteen, made
    treats,
In flew a canary, now they serve shredded tweets.
For dinner they served up roast parrot for meat,
Now their customers' tummies Repeat and Repeat
and repeat   and repeat   and repeat . . . . . .

SPOT

He had spots, boils and dimples mixed in with
    his wrinkles,
He had warts and carbuncles and numerous
    pimples,
From a chemist he knew he asked, 'What shall I
    do?'
She said, 'Vanishing cream, it's so simple.'

So he bought a large pot and applied the whole
    lot,
And he looked in the mirror to see what he'd got,
His face disappeared as he peered at his grots,
So he'll never know now if he's rid of his spots.

TWADDLE

Some called him a squirrel, some called him
    magpie,
He would buy, sell or barter if a thing caught his
    eye,
His cupboards and shelves and the lofts in the
    house,
Were full to the gunnels which made his wife
    grouse.

'Get rid of that camera and the stupid dark room,
To give us some space, so please sell it and soon.'
So his sales list was written and placed in the
    'Ads',
For one infra red camera from Burpstein Hasblad'.

The large Eyesaw lens made by Skooter is new,
With Hydroscope shutter of which there are two,
Calibrated from nought to zero and back,
It's Millennium compliant, with black camera
    pack.

The light marked 'B.F.', warns of triple exposure,
There's an Infinite Snoggler against decomposure,
The camera takes most films and with 'Auto-
    reverse',
This doubles the photos upon the obverse.

His wife didn't know that the 'Ad' was all
    twaddle,
Photographers knew that there was no such model,

And so such a sale – it was never to be,
Now they live in the garage. It's the one room
    that's free.

WEBSITE

Pring, Pring, Pring, Pring, went the telephone ring,
I've a long distance call for some guy,
I eye, I eye, I eye, said the fly,
I'm just on the web, don't ask why.

Now the spider was home and he picked up the
    phone,
Saying 'Fly is tied up for a while.'
I'm not spinning a yarn, the fly is now calm.
He's to join me for dinner in style.

The spider had six flies for dinner that day,
Web sites are a lucrative source,
Internet's a connection that no fly should make,
For they're not the main guest, they're main
    course.

YAKERTY YAK

Yakerty, Yakerty Yak,
I've decided to give her the sack.
Her head goes in first,
Or perhaps the reverse,
Then the end with the head I will wack.

Wakerty, Wakerty wak,
At last I have got my own back.
She'll no longer carp,
Whilst she's playing her harp,
But I bet she'll still Yakerty Yak.